Read-About® Geography

Texas

By Carmen Bredeson

Consultant
Linda Cornwell
National Literacy Specialist

Children's Press®
A Division of Scholastic Inc.
New York   Toronto   London   Auckland   Sydney
Mexico City   New Delhi   Hong Kong
Danbury, Connecticut

Designer: Herman Adler Design
Photo Researcher: Caroline Anderson
The photo on the cover shows the Rio Grande.

Library of Congress Cataloging-in-Publication Data

Bredeson, Carmen.
    Texas / by Carmen Bredeson
      p. cm. — (Rookie read-about geography)
    Includes index.
    Summary: An introduction to the land and people of the state of Texas.
    ISBN 0-516-22270-8 (lib. bdg.)   0-516-27393-0 (pbk.)
    1. Texas—Juvenile literature. [1. Texas.] I. Title. II. Series.
  F386.3.B74   2002
  976.4—dc21

2001005754

The name "Texas" (TEK-suhs) comes from the Spanish word *tejas* (TAY-hoss), which means friend.

Texas is a big, friendly state. It is the second largest state in the United States. Only Alaska (uh-LASS-kuh) is bigger.

CANADA

WASHINGTON

OREGON

IDAHO

MONTANA

NORTH DAKOTA

SOUTH DAKOTA

WYOMING

NEBRASKA

NEVADA

UTAH

COLORADO

KANSAS

CALIFORNIA

ARIZONA

NEW MEXICO

OKLAHOMA

TEXAS

MINNESOTA

WISCONSIN

IOWA

MICHIGAN

ILLINOIS

INDIANA

MISSOURI

ARKANSAS

LOUISIANA

MISSISSIPPI

ALABAMA

TENNESSEE

KENTUCKY

OHIO

WEST VIRGINIA

VIRGINIA

NORTH CAROLINA

SOUTH CAROLINA

GEORGIA

FLORIDA

NEW HAMPSHIRE

VERMONT

MAINE

NEW YORK

PENNSYLVANIA

MASSACHUSETTS

RHODE ISLAND

CONNECTICUT

NEW JERSEY

DELAWARE

MARYLAND

Washington, D.C.

North

West   East

South

ALASKA   CANADA

MEXICO

HAWAII

5

There are many farms in Texas. Some farmers grow rice, oranges, or cotton.

When cotton is ready to be picked, the fields turn white.

There are also many ranches in Texas. Ranchers raise animals instead of crops.

Some ranchers raise
sheep, goats, or cattle.

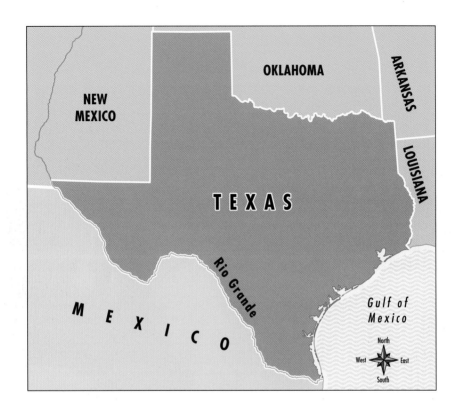

Mexico (MEK-si-koh) is the country next to Texas. Most people in Mexico speak Spanish.

The sandy beaches of Texas curve along the Gulf of Mexico.

The Rio Grande
(ree-oh-GRAND) flows
between Texas and Mexico.

Rio Grande means "big
river" in Spanish. It is the
longest river in Texas.

Alligators, mountain lions, rattlesnakes, and lizards are some of the wild animals that live in Texas.

The horned lizard looks like a tiny dinosaur!

Austin is the capital
of Texas. The capital
is where the state
government makes laws.

The city of Austin was named after Stephen F. Austin. He is called the "Father of Texas" because he formed the first American town in Texas.

19

Texans have many different jobs. Some Texans work in oil refineries.

Refineries turn oil
into gasoline.

Some Texans even fly
in outer space. They are
called astronauts.

These astronauts learn to
work in space at NASA
in Houston.

Many Texans enjoy sports.
Some football fans cheer
for the Dallas Cowboys.

Lots of basketball fans watch the Houston Rockets.

Rodeos (ROH-dee-ohz)
are also popular in Texas.

Cowboys and cowgirls
try to ride bucking horses
and bulls. The animals
usually throw their riders
to the ground.

Maybe you can visit Texas someday. There is a lot to do in this great big state!

Words You Know

astronauts

Austin

cotton

mountain lion

oil refinery

rancher

Rio Grande

rodeo

Index

About the Author

Carmen Bredeson is the author of twenty-five books for children.
She lives in Texas and enjoys doing research and traveling.

Photo Credits

Photographs © 2002: AP/Wide World Photos: 25 (Tim Johnson), 24 (Tim
Sharp); Archive Photos/Getty Images: 19, 30 top right; Bruce Coleman Inc.:
11, 13, 31 bottom left (Matt Bradley), 16 (John Elk III), 23 (Stouffer Enterprises);
Buddy Mays/Travel Stock: 28; Dave G. Houser/HouserStock, Inc.: 8; Minden
Pictures: cover (Carr Clifton), 14, 30 bottom right (Tim Fitzharris); Peter
Arnold Inc.: 9, 31 top right (H.R. Bramaz), 20, 31 top left (Jim Olive); Photo
Researchers, NY: 27, 31 bottom right (Jerry Irwin), 22, 30 top left (NASA/SPL);
Superstock, Inc.: 3; The Image Works/Bob Daemmrich: 6, 7, 21, 30 bottom left;
Visuals Unlimited/Joe McDonald: 15.

Maps by Bob Italiano